Take Courage, My Daughter
A Journey of Resilience and Faith

BY
JANICE LINDER

I received your book today, I didn't realize your hardships in your life besides for Bill and raising your children in problems you had with your ex-husband. I am truly sorry for your struggles but you are my inspiration I'm very proud of who you've become and how you've always stood by God and never turned your back on him. thank you for being you I love you.

Misty Lagrou

Printed in the United States of America

ISBN 979-8-89114-088-2 (sc)
ISBN 979-8-89114-090-5 (e)

Library of Congress Control Number: 2024910451

2024.06.26

MainSpring Books
5901 W. Century Blvd
Suite 750
Los Angeles, CA, US, 90045

www.mainspringbooks.com

PREFACE

I grew up in Bellingham Washington where I was born and raised. I had a wonderful childhood. I have 3 siblings. My sister is 3 and 1/2 years older than me, then I'm next, my brothers are 6 years and 8 years younger than me.

My dad built two of the homes for us, one in Acme, WA and one in Evans Washington. My dad was a master builder. We moved a lot. I would say 36 different homes throughout my childhood.

We did not have a TV growing up. We played outside until it got dark, we always lived at least 20 to 30 miles out of town. There was a lot of music in our house. My mom played the piano and stand-up bass and still does to this day. We would surround the piano and sing, my dad, mom, sister and I sang.

I don't remember my little brother's ever singing. But today my brother who is 6 years younger than me is a pastor and plays the guitar and sings at his church. God has given me an anointed voice when I sing and I have been on worship teams since I was 19 years old. My style is country. I sound like Patsy Cline. I do sing her songs.

When I was 6 years old, we lived in Spokane Washington and I sang on the local TV channel.

And when I was in my thirties, I did a lot of specials at a church that I was on the local channel before the pastor preaching in Pocatello Idaho.

I recorded my first CD in 2017, my long-time desire.

Life was good on the farm. We always had barn animals, we milked cows, we had beef cows, chickens and turkeys. And we always had an acre of garden to pull weeds and get fruit and vegetables. I remember staying home from school to butcher chickens. We would do 100 in one day. I was the one who cut them, and put them in the freezer.

My Mom and Grandma passed on being a great cook down to me. I enjoy cooking and baking.

I am a good cook, my children say.

When my kids were growing up, we always ate together at night time and on Fridays we always had game night, that's how I felt like we were a normal family between the abuse and the trauma.

People say that I have become the woman that I am today because of what I've gone through in life, I don't know if I agree with that, I didn't ask for the abuse. I have lived in Washington, Idaho, Montana, North Dakota, Wyoming and also Alaska. I guess you could say I am a little bit of a traveler. But in reality, I always thought if I moved to a new place that it would be better, but the reality is your baggage and your trauma still follows you wherever you go.

CHAPTER 1
MY STORY, MY WORDS

We all have stories to tell…. My story starts on a Thursday mid July 1960 words spoken to me we're not positive I remember going to kindergarten I cried I didn't want to go. We lived on a dairy farm in Whatcom County Washington. My sister was in second grade and I believe my mom was pregnant at that time. I am told the first grade was rough. Oh, I didn't know what to do and put my head on the desk. Needless to say, I took first grade over again. From the nurses from birth to teachers to family members they started a long downward effect. I was told that I was dumb, not good enough in school. I was told that until my 10th year of school, when I was in a special English class, the teacher saw potential in me. I had a hard time reading so from Reading to my brain to put it on paper there was a short. My teacher saw that. I would study and take tests in her room. She would read the questions to me and I would answer the questions. I went from an F to c and b. Now it has a name, dyslexia instead of stupid dumb can't learn. I have dealt with that all my life. I was not encouraged to do what I wanted to be, a nurse I was left with the only thing you would be good at is a wife and a mother. That's what I heard. One of the biggest lies of my life.

1st grade came and went, I wasn't ready for first grade either. I started first grade again for the second time, things were going a little better as I remember. What I didn't know at the time until years later I have a learning disability and still do. Dyslexia is a disease you can't see. It has stopped me from doing a lot of things I wanted to do and was told I can't do. I had teachers and other students tell me that I was dumb and wouldn't amount to anything. So I believed what others said about me.

We always lived in the country, we lived at least 20 miles out of town, but because we lived in the country, I remember playing outside in the barn making hay forts and swinging on a homemade swing. I remember coming inside to take a bath, boy did that hurt from all the scratches on my legs and arms. Those were wonderful memories.

When I was about 12 years old, we were living in a little town of Acme, WA. We were lived by family friends, their daughter and son in law. I trusted so called Christians, one day when the wife was gone the husband took me upstairs and started to fondle me and wanted me to do the same to him. I don't remember all the details because I blocked the memories, but what I remember is that I was scared to death, he was touching places he shouldn't have and didn't want to be there. This man told me to not tell anyone what he did to me. It was a little bit of time before I told someone, it came to find out I wasn't the only little girl he fondled. A short time later the wife divorced him.

That was the start of being scared of the opposite sex. As a teenager I didn't trust the males, even when I started to date which wasn't much. I remember when I did go on a date, I would act like I was sleeping when he brought me home. Thinking back to when I was 6 years old when I kissed the first boy behind the school house. So innocent I was.

CHAPTER 2
FAMILY THAT ISN'T BLOOD

We moved to Colville, WA when I was 17 and went to a Christian school a little different from coming from a public school for 10 years. I was told to leave 6 feet from me and the boys. I got in trouble all the time talking to the boys. At the school I met friends that would be lifetime friends of over 40 years now. Becky and Richy Olson and their parents became my adopted family.

I remember quite often I was at their house, I was asked why I was at their house all the time, my answer was I don't know! Why I was there all the time, I felt loved and welcomed, a part of the family. I remember them ordering taco burgers and Pepsi. You see Becky got me liking Pepsi. At my house we didn't get to eat out, alone have soda. We didn't get junk food, for the food we ate we grew. We always had a garden and an acre of land for food. We had chickens, milk cows, pigs, turkeys, and beef cows. My dad worked hard and long hours. My mom would bake bread and goodies. So, we ate what was in the garden or the animals we raised.

There were only 3 kids at home, my older sister was married, I am the second child, a brother who is 6 years younger and my baby brother 8 years younger than me.

I was 18 and babysitting in town for my friend's sister and brother-in-law. I was living with them in an apartment above the IGA grocery store. There were sheets as a door, where I was staying in the living room so I could hear the baby. One morning when the wife was at work the husband cornered me in the kitchen between the counters.

It was a L shape. I had nowhere to go, so I was trapped. He said "I am fixed so you won't get pregnant." The balls of him to come on to me. He kept asking me and I kept telling him NO. he even would buy me beer so I would sleep with him. After a couple of weeks being scared of him, I told the wife that I had to leave, I couldn't babysit anymore and told her why I was leaving.

CHAPTER 3
THE GUY I STOOD UP

My mom and dads' friends had 4 boys. One of the boys called and asked me out. I said yes but after we hung up, I realized it was the wrong brother I wanted to go out with. So, when it came to going out, I was so scared I stayed under my bed when he came to pick me up. My family left for the evening. I was so scared it seemed like hours I was under that bed. I felt bad but we never said anything about that night. He moved away shortly after that. I will be talking about him later.

CHAPTER 4
MY INNOCENT GONE

I was 19 and was working at a restaurant as an assistant Chef. I fell for the chief, the worldly man that he was just out of the Navy at 21. I liked him a lot. We started to become friends it was fun working with Rick. Since I lived 45 minutes from home. I stayed at the motel that was behind the restaurant. My parents said I could work there because my aunt, my mom's sister, was the manager there. One night we were having a drink, one too many, we went to his room where he was staying also. Famous last words "don't worry nothing will happen", he took my most valued part of me, my virginity without my permission. I was totally out cold from the drinking, woke up in a puddle of blood. I felt dirty unclean, every other word you can add I felt even God didn't want me. So, this is where Satan came in and speaking in your ears and I believed all the lies. I wasn't going to be having sex until I got married" "nothing will happen" bull crap he lied. I was so ashamed I didn't go home for two weeks. My parents came to see if I was ok and why I didn't come home. The owner of the place told them I was staying in one of the rooms behind the restaurant which was true but I can't tell them the truth. I felt dirty, unclean and ashamed of letting that happen to me. Rick wanted to move in together, a couple of weeks later we got a house. I felt dirty and my mom's words ring in my ears" you made your bed you have to lay in it" I thought why not. That didn't last long. Rick quit his job at the restaurant that left me just working. That lasted 2 months and I called my dad to come and get me and I moved home.

CHAPTER 5
DODGE A BULLET

I was seeing a nice man from church and told him what happened to me, it seemed ok with him, and that it wasn't my fault. It had been a couple of months that we were seeing each other when we were looking at rings. He did ask me to marry him, I said yes. I was happy but what I didn't know was that he would have been a controller, he would have told me what to wear and who I could see and how to dress. Sure, dodged that bullet but that was not the worst of it he told me... he rejected me. I was not a virgin, I was unclean, damaged goodies, used and that's how I was feeling, and it was an arrow straight through my heart. It didn't matter that he would masturbate and that was ok but he rejected me, and abandoned me. I had no idea how long I would carry that around with me and it was for 48 years ...what is wrong with me, am I so unlovable? I was looking for love, someone to love me, someone to accept me. At the time I didn't know that's what I was looking for. My self-worth was nothing. I saw myself as damaged. I know what you are thinking BUT GOD... this man wasn't God's best for me but it started a disorder in me that lasted for 40 years looking for approval, to be loved by a man.

That fall, my thoughts of suicide was the way I could make things better, all I had to do was walk out to the water and keep walking and never stop. So, you see my best friend, her sister and I were camping so it would have been easy. Someone took something from me and I couldn't get back. My innocence, my childhood but I look back today and one thing I know is that my GOD was with me always. That's why I didn't walk into that water. Satan knew that God had something wonderful for me in store. The rejection of a man put me in a tailspin for many years. I didn't know until a couple of years ago why it felt like I was spinning out of control. With God's help I figured it out and why I picked the wrong men. I am a fixer, I take on the role of a mother and love them through the pain and circumstances they are dealing with. I am a nurturer. I felt deserted which I didn't know until years later. I just knew I was empty inside looking for something for years. I felt people let me down and didn't love me even my own family members. The only thing I knew was my daddy loved me and my heavenly father loved me but that wasn't enough.

At the age of 8 years old I would carry my brothers on my hips, one on one side and the other on the other hip. I remember I would bring my brothers with me when I would come into town to meet my friends, they would ask me why do you need to bring them with you, I would always tell them because I want to.

CHAPTER 6
CHASING A DREAM

I have been chasing a vision that my mom of a blond-haired guy with the part on the left side. I have been looking for that perfect man who would love me and I could be safe, I am still waiting for that man in the vision my mom had. It took me 53 years to realize I don't need a man to make me happy and whole. I thought my happiness lay in being married and being a mother. That's what my mom said I would only be good at. That's what I heard, I could only be a good wife and mother. Well, I got one thing right.... Being a mom is what I have done well and loved every minute. You see I wasn't encouraged to be what I wanted to be, I wanted to be a nurse since I was 9 years old, so at 51 I was taking classes online to go into nursing school and my mom told me to quit school" you can't do it, you wouldn't be able to make it through to be a nurse" I quit because they said I couldn't do it. Why do I do what others say to do or just say I can't do It. That's the big question! I know now what her intentions were so I wouldn't fail. That was their way of protecting me.

Why don't we just listen to our heavenly father and how he sees us, what is our worth. Time and time again, he has told me that I was his daughter and saw me as a precious gem, and he loves me. I was white as snow. Don't get me wrong I had a wonderful loving dad who I knew loved me. But there was something missing. Instead, I was looking for a man to fill that hole.

CHAPTER 7

THE D-WORD

I was home for about 9 months when my mom put me on a bus sending me to my sisters. I didn't know at the time why but my sister and I found out 2 months later she was divorcing my dad of 25 years of marriage. As I was leaving, my dad was saying goodbye to me and crying, I can still see him to this day. I am my daddy's little girl. That was an awful day not knowing why my mom was sending me away at the age of 19. Rejection again now from my mom. She was leaving with another woman who convinced her she needed to leave her family to be with her. Looking back today I wish I was left alone to stay with my dad and brothers. We could have had a dairy farm but it didn't happen. My brothers were too young and didn't want a dairy farm. My dad and brothers moved to where my sister and I were, Everson, WA. I gave up my little apartment to get a house for the 4 of us, so I could help take care of my brothers. I am 20 now trying to figure out my life. What were my desires? I didn't know and now I had to help with my brothers who were 12 and 14.

That only lasted a couple of months when my aunt, my dad's sister found a woman for my dad. They were dating for a little bit when my dad would run and hide from this woman, you see this woman was not a very nice lady. She seduced my dad and he felt that he had to marry her. I begged my dad not to marry her. This person had 2 children still at home, for me to take care of while they went to Hawaii for 2 weeks on their honeymoon. Her daughters begged my dad not to marry their mom. While they were gone, I turned 21 and had no idea what was going to happen. All hell broke loose when she got back home. She expected me to be her maid. She called me

Cindy for Cinderella. This woman was the ugly stepmother in the story of Cinderella, no lie, But the 2 step sisters were wonderful people. She said to me "I kicked my kids out at 18 and you should be lucky you are still here". I left about 2 weeks later. I was staying on couches, I went house to house, four homes until I went to Libby, MT. I am so thankful for the family in Montana who took me in again, my best friend Becky.

A year later my dad divorced his wife and wanted me to come to Spokane, WA to take care of him {second time} we went to Colville, WA for a couple of months. We were staying at my uncle property until we left to go to Spokane. My dad's x wife found out where he was living and was going trying to get in the trailer and wait for him until he got home, I was in the trailer with a gun pointed at her as she was climbing though the little widow, I hated this woman with all my heart for what she said to me and trapping my dad. I didn't want to be there but I stayed here until my dad got home. I called some friends to come and get me so I could stay somewhere for a couple of days. This woman told me I had to leave. I am a doormat I would always do what people wanted. This woman is a black widow. Her own children said she killed their father.

I made a mistake to go home with that guy that I stood up on that date years earlier. Well, he was married and seemed to care about what was going on at the time, I thought. The couple drugged me and took pictures and raped me for 4 days. They both took advantage of me. I remember trying all my might to stop him but I couldn't. Later, I thought he was getting back at me for standing him up years earlier. Years later I found out that the couple did the same thing to my cousin, our stories were the same. Shortly after this happened my dad and I left for Spokane. I never told my dad what happened, my dad went to his grave without knowing.

My dad was milking cows in the morning and at night at a farm in Spokane. We lived in a little house on the farm. Things were going good when the x wife would leave notes on my dad's car saying, we were here and what we were doing. She is a sick mental person and passed away as a mental person.

CHAPTER 8
BILL THE CHARMING CON-ARTIST

I was 23 now and went jogging one day along the road and met this nice-looking young man, a charming con man, he was working in his yard. Bill said to me if I wanted to come back and help after my run. I didn't know anyone in the neighborhood. I was so lost and wanted to be loved, I started seeing him and I would invite him back to my house while my dad was at work. I would wait for him all night and he wouldn't show up. I spent a lot of time at his mom and dad's house because he still lived at home. Bill was only 19 and had no job. I should have known it would be a bad thing to get involved with him. No job and I had to pay for our first date but I was in love with this guy or I thought I was. WHAT IS LOVE!! Bill asked me to ask my dad to buy him a car ...

I asked and my dad bought it, boy like dummies we did what he asked. He said he would pay my dad back in 2 payments but that didn't happen, so my dad went and picked the car up and later my dad would trade it in. I would say it was about 2 months later I found out I was pregnant with our 1st child. I told Bill and his family that I was pregnant and didn't want anything from him, just for him to be there for me. Bill ran about 2 weeks later. Bill left town hitch hiking across the US states. He left for eight months and returned 2 weeks before our first daughter was born.

It took me a little while to tell my dad I was pregnant, and when I did, he told me that I needed to get an abortion, that I was going to ruin my life by having this child, that I wanted and needed so much. Someone to love me and I could love, someone of my own. I told my dad that I wouldn't do that, I couldn't do that. I was almost 24 at this time. I wanted and needed this baby. I needed someone to love me unconditionally who I could love and be loved. We moved to a bigger house off of the farm just down the road with another bedroom for the new baby. Things were going good I thought, well I left for the weekend and when I came back I found out that my dad got remarried to that mental woman. That woman kicked me out of the house that my dad and I were sharing. So, here I was pregnant and kicked out of my father's house for the second time. I am surprised I didn't hate my dad, here we go again rejected by another man.

Bill's mom helped me get on my feet and get into a place. Thinking back, I was about three weeks before the baby was to be born. He came back and his mother told me I needed to take him back and try to make a family with him. I didn't want him at all but doing the right thing and trying to do the right thing was hard. we both didn't want each other at least the baby would have a mom and a dad. I knew it was a mistake. He was a sweet talker and a con man. It was time to have this baby. but at the time I was doing things with his brother and he stepped aside so I could try to make a life with his brother.

Bill and now my own father. No wonder I have a rejection problem with people. I know I did things backwards but I was so glad to have this baby that was growing in my belly. I already loved this child and dreamed about our lives together. It came time to have this baby, I was in labor for 16 hours.

When Amanda was about 9 months old. Bill and I were going to go to the courthouse and get married but it was about 2 weeks later when Bill left for his journey across the States again, we didn't get married.

I felt abandoned, left, unworthy to be someone's wife. As I was watching him walk away heading down the road, I was thinking now what, he just left me with a 9 months old baby girl to raise her by myself. Amanda Joy was a wonderful baby and an amazing daughter.

Bill said he always found a girl who looked like me or was pregnant to hook up with along his way to and from me. Well that lasted for seven years and 3 more living kids, a miscarriage and a stillborn baby boy who didn't make it to take his first breath of air. Bill was with me for every birth even for my baby boy that I was 38 weeks along. For seven years he came and went out of our lives. I think he came back every year, I would get pregnant, Jessica was next and 18 months after I had Kristofer, then 2 years later Jeremy came alone. So, after the last child was born, I decided I better do something about it and not have any more children. It was kind of funny when I was 19 the doctor told me I would never have kids, I guess I showed him. Bill always knew when I was going to give birth, he would head for home about a week before giving birth and then would leave again. I know what you are thinking WHY did I have so many kids and why did I wait for him to come back. I wanted to be loved and I knew he would be back. When my last child was one and half, I told Bill to leave and not come back, I had it with him coming and going.

My dad never stood up to this woman in the 20 some years he was married to her. My dad passed away after having open heart surgery as a result of being poisoned by his wife. She was a RN nurse and had access to drugs and poison. The black widow.

CHAPTER 9
THE MAN I MARRIED

I never imagined how my life and my children's lives would change in the way that it did. I met a guy from church, I fell in love with this man or was it lust. This person had baggage, he told me he had a Pandora box, what is a Pandora box anyway and that I didn't know I would have to deal with. Just because someone goes to church and his mom is involved in the church doesn't mean he is a Christian. The fruits were not there and that was another sign but I was in love with him. My family told me not to marry him, but I chased him and talked him into marrying me. He really didn't want to but I thought I could love him enough to make up for him not taking that leap of faith we would be okay. What I didn't know was that he was sleeping with other women besides me. We dated for 2 years. He moved to Alaska for a job, I should have left things alone looking back now. His mom didn't like me or didn't dislike me. She thought that her son shouldn't have to support my kids, when my kid's dad didn't pay any support. I talked this man into marrying me in Alaska, boy should I have not gone. Seven months after we were married, he told me that I should divorce him, I told him no way he wasn't going to get out of it that easily. You see I left my kids with my brother and sister-in law until we could move somewhere where we could have the kids. We were on a little island in the bearing sea, not the ideal for kids to live there, he told me.

I moved back to where my family was in Washington and then about 4 months later my kids and I left for Nome Alaska. Life was good there but then we moved to Pocatello, Id about 9 months later, he didn't want to move but he was thinking we could move back with a pay raise. It never happened that we moved back to Alaska. All hell broke loose about 5 years after being there. If it wasn't one thing it was another. We started to fight and he would call me all kinds of names, that's where the abuse started verbal, mental, sexual, emotional and physical. He would belittle me, things got bad and it was spilling over to my kids. I didn't know it at that time, it was 5 of us that were getting abused and not just me. I was living in my own safe place in my mind. I wasn't living life, I was surviving. What I found out over the 18 years of leaving four times and coming back, you can't make someone love you and want to be with you. This person loved only his narcissistic self and the other women he was sleeping with.

CHAPTER 10

JESSICA

Jessica, my second daughter, the second child. She ran away at the age of 15 years old. Her now in-laws paid for her to take a bus 10 hours away without my permission. I looked for her for 2 years, no one would let me know where she was. I asked Debbie and Mark Hudspeth (Jessica's in-laws) but they wouldn't tell me where she was. I asked my dad's wife who lied where she was. There were 5 people who were involved in hiding her. She followed her boyfriend at the time back home to fruit land, Washington. Jessica left me a note on her pillow. Telling me she loved me and needed to go. She told me that she was not feeling very well so she went to bed and then left through the window and hid in the bushes so we wouldn't see her. My other kids and I looked for hours for her but Jessica was gone. Just days before I put your boyfriend on the bus to go home and she wanted to leave with him. I told her that she had to stay with her family. I still have that note that she wrote to me. I know now why she left. My husband at the time was an abusive man. Un- knows to me he abused my children also. I cried for 2 years for Jessica.

I remember I had to travel 10 hours to a court date for Jessica. I was sitting in the courtroom feeling like a criminal wanting to hold my daughter and bring her home. The judge ruled that she wouldn't be coming home with me, I was heartbroken, and cried all the way home to Idaho. My last thoughts and seeing her getting into a cop car being taken away., not what a mom wants to see.

Things got bad, each year the abuse would escalate from the year before. So, my kids and I left Pocatello Id for Grants Pass, Or to a safe place where my best friend lived and I knew we would have a place to live and I would have a job at the end of the long trip. After 2 years of missing Jessica, I reached out to her, she was 17 now. I sent a plane ticket to Jessica to come to Oregon to have Christmas with me and her siblings, Jessica's boyfriend, mom and dad told her that it was a trap, for Pete's sake I was her mother and still Legally responsible for Jessica. I talked to her on the phone and told her, we loved her and wanted her to come for Christmas with no strings attached. Jessica came to Oregon to spend Christmas with us. Two weeks later Jessica called me to come and get her. I went to Washington and picked her up. That didn't last about 2 weeks. When she went back, her boyfriend came to pick her up and take her back to Washington. I had a talk with her boyfriend and said that I loved her more than he did but if he was going to take her back with him, he had to marry her.

Joe and Jessica were married 2 months later. We headed up to the wedding. At the wedding Jessica' s new soon to be mother in-law was in control of everything, I was the ugly red headed step child. I was nothing. She was the mother of the bride and she let everyone know. That's where it started dealing with the in-laws from hell. Twist and turns I have had to endure these people and still have too, we are grandparents together. Only by the Grace of God I can stand them. They are still causing trouble to this day, for Jessica and Joe and I.

My life hasn't been very easy, with the other grandparents, the first two grandkids were not too bad when they were born because they lived a couple of hours away but when Dilya, the third grandchild was born, the other grandparents told me "The GRANDPARENTS were there so I could leave and go home". Steam was coming out of my ears. I always spent 2 weeks with my daughters and helped them with the babies and with her. These people always talked crap about me and my family. It's been a trial for 22 years. They feel like it's a competition and they need to win. After all this mess my relationship with my daughter and grandkids is strong.

CHAPTER 11
I WENT BACK TO IDAHO

Jeremy wanted to move back to Idaho because he missed Dave, the only dad he knew. This man loved our dogs more than me. I was there for 2 years before I left. In the months before I left for the last time he was drunk like always, he put a 9mm gun in my face and told me that he wouldn't cry because I was just a human and I didn't matter but if he shot our dogs, he would cry a little because he loved them. Then he turned the gun to my son and said the same thing that he said to me. I looked at my son and said I will see you in heaven, not knowing if Dave would pull the trigger. I slept with my gun under my pillow and said I will see you in heaven, not knowing if I would need to use it. I never knew if I would live or die that night. I won't go into any details of the abuse but I think you can imagine. They are too bad to tell you. I should have called the cops but in the mind set I was, I couldn't do anything.

September of 2008 I was losing blood for 4 months. So, I went to the doctor to ask for a hysterectomy and she told me to just wait for a little bit. One morning I woke up and I knew that I needed to get to the ER, so I went to the clinic because it was less expensive than going to the hospital. When I got to the clinic the doctor tried to take my blood pressure and he couldn't find it, I laid down, sat up, he still couldn't find it, he asked who drove me to the clinic and I said nobody I drove myself. He called the ER and told them that I was on my way and they were waiting for me. I called my oldest daughter to talk to me on the way to the hospital, so I wouldn't pass out. Got to the ER and I got right in, the ER doctor stayed by my side while they got a room ready upstairs. I had four units of blood that day.

And had two more the day of the surgery. My doctor came into the ER and told me she was sorry for not listening to me and having a hysterectomy. For I had been bleeding and losing blood for 4 months prior to this. I told my husband at the time that I had to have units of blood and he said it was all in my head.

Two days after my surgery this idiot told me that I needed to go and get him booze down at the liquor store, I drove to the liquor store, got him his booze, came back and went to bed. I shouldn't have been driving. I could barely function. I was heavily medicated.

A few weeks after the surgery he took me down to a lawyer to get separation papers so he didn't have to be responsible for my hospital bills, he didn't put me on his health insurance. The lawyer asked if I wanted something in the papers so when he divorced me, I would get money from him but the state of mind that I was in I couldn't tell the lawyer what was going on. Dave didn't care about me it was all about him.

God told me that I needed to leave. My kids were scared for safety because he would have killed me. On the last day I decided to leave he peed on me and thought that it was funny, I told him that I was gone and I did desire someone better than him. I left 15-years ago. Thank the lord I broke that curse. I went to go live with my second daughter and her family in Montana.

Jessica and the kids and I moved to North Dakota. That's where Joe was working at the time. He was coming home every other weekend to Montana. While we lived in ND, I went to the therapist because I was mentally unwell, not healthy at all. She said that I had PTSD from my ex-husband with the trauma and all the abuse.

My little angel when Dilya was 18 months old. She knew that I needed her. My state of mind wasn't good, I was so damaged mentally. I was going down the same path as before years ago but this time, I was deeply depressed and had anxiety. She did not leave my side she stroked my hair and she loved on me. I thought suicide was the best opinion of how I felt. I never told anyone how I really felt. I kept everything bottled deep down. I still haven't really told my whole story.

This little angel saved my life. We have a special bond she is my doodlebug. We still have a special relationship to this day. My daughter told me that she believes that she had Dilyla for me.

CHAPTER 12

JEREMY

Jeremy, my baby, the fourth child, was in a motor bike accident. That call all parents fear. "Got the call your boy was in a motor bike accident and we don't know if he will make, get here" I was 3.5 hours away in Montana he was in Idaho. June 15, 2010 will be in mind forever. One of my worst days of my life. Every half hour the nurse or doctor called to see where we were and get here soon. When we made it to Pocatello ID, Jeremy just got out of surgery. Jeremy was having his scalp scraped from rocks and his right ear repaired from it tearing off half way. The doctors told me that they didn't know what was broken and if he would die or even last though the night. The doctors said that he might be vegetable for the rest of his life. Jeremy was on life support and put in a induce coma in ICU. They didn't know how bad Jeremy was. Before this time our relationship was strained for one year and seven months, I haven't seen or talked to him.

Needless to say, I was heartbroken. There is a funny in this tragedy, I had to sneak into town without my x husband knowing. My kids and I where 4 houses away down the street. I would let the homeowners know when I was down the road and they would open the garage doors and I would drive in and they closed the doors.

When I got to the ICU, I saw Jeremy and I started praying from his head to his toes. I prayed for God's healing and power over him to mend the bones and muscles. The power of prayers. When you don't have the words, the holy spirit spoke for me. There my baby was laying with bandages on his head, tubes in his mouth, tubes out of his sides, road rash on his arms. I told Jeremy that I loved him so much and that I was here. About 4 am the next day the nurse told me to come to Jeremy's room, that Jeremy was awake and wanted to see me. Miracle 1, he woke up. Not brain dead. Jeremy got a piece of paper and wrote on it, "Hi I love you Mom". I was so overwhelmed and cried. Jeremy is a walking miracle. A semi-truck with 2 trailers full of gravel ran over him and drugged him 30 feet and she didn't even know it. She was taking up all four lanes and Jeremy was going too fast. Jeremy just saw a program on how to survive a motorbike accident. Jeremy used the info on what to do. Jeremy rode on top of the bike that was on its side siding under the semi. The tires ran over him. Jeremy was running home on his lunch hour to take his dog out to go potty. Jeremy wasn't wearing a helmet and he was in shorts.

The cops and paramedics didn't know who he was or how old he was at the scene of the crash. Jeremy made the front page of the paper and national news. Jeremy was in IUC for 3 days. Jeremy broke 9 of his ribs front and back, pelvis, punctured lung and bruised lungs, broken clavicle, road rash and 90% blind in his right eye. We are praying for his healing, and later said that he broke his wrist. God is so good. At the time of the accident Jeremy and his wife Irene were separated and now they have 3 kids.

As of today, I haven't had a relationship with Jeremy and my grandkids for 5 years because of a jealous girl who doesn't want her husband and kids to have a relationship with me. I am an awful grandma in her eyes. I didn't take enough pictures of her kids and I loved my other grandkids more than hers.

I am not defined by what has happened to me and what my mind set was but I am a child of God and he loves me.

I didn't go into all the details of my life but just the highlights. That will be a couple more stories to tell.

Thank you for reading this and may the lord be with you and bless you. What got me though was my God, many go to the bottle or do drugs but God walked with me even when I thought he wasn't there, but he was.

There is hope, you are not alone like I thought I was. My God didn't leave me or forsake me. People say "what happened to me has shaped me" but I didn't ask for the abuse. I just wanted to be loved. We need to take what some people say with a grain of salt. Because if they haven't been where you are, they have no way of knowing how you feel. And it's ok not being okay.

I have four beautiful children who are all grown up and have their own children. I am blessed to have them and 10 grandchildren. Just to let you know I haven't found anyone special yet.

Amanda Joy you are my joy in life, you are an amazing mom and friend. She helps deliver babies.

I can't imagine not having you as my beautiful daughter. I Love you

Jessica Anne, you are one of my best friends. You are an amazing mom and human being. I am so proud of you, for what a beautiful person you are inside and out. I Love you

Kristofer Donald you are my rock who has been there for and with me, you are amazing human beings. I am so proud of you. I love you

Jeremy Paul, you are my inspiration. I love you.

Kathy and Don: Thank you for loving me and not judging me.

Becky: Thank you for always being there when I needed you.

Richy: Thank you for the loving hugs that I needed.

Forgiveness was my key to healing.

You need to forgive yourself and them for you.

I wrote out on paper everyone who I needed to forgive, wrote what I needed to forgive them for and signed it and prayed that God would help me forgive them and give it to him and never take it back.

It has been freeing for me, I have not taken it back. My pile of forgiveness papers are thick.

This was my life line, I kept it in my heart for hope.

Jeremiah 29:11-14a

For I know the plans I have for you, declares the Lord. "Plans to prosper you and not harm you, plans to give you hope and a future.

Then you will call upon me and come and pray to me, I will listen to you.

You will seek me and find me when you seek me with all your heart.

I will be found by you" declares the Lord"

I am strong mentally and physically now with God's help.

Dear Janice,

I will never leave you or never forsake you

God your father, your daddy

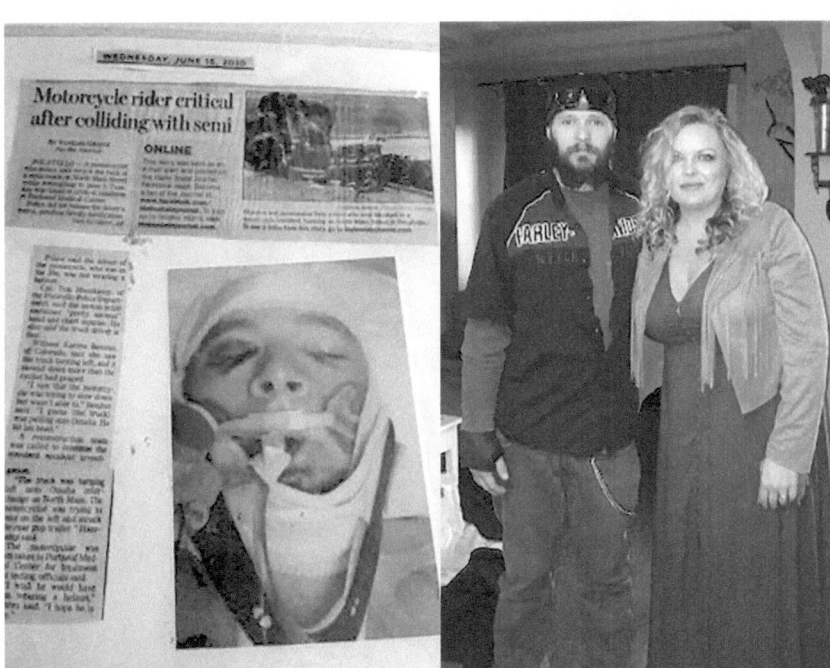